A MACDONALD BOOK

Text © 1988 Angela Littler
Illustrations © 1988 Macdonald & Co (Publishers) Ltd

First published in Great Britain in 1988
by Macdonald & Co (Publishers) Ltd
London & Sydney

A member of Maxwell Pergamon Publishing Corporation plc

Printed and bound in Spain by Cronion S.A.

ISBN 0 356 13496 2
ISBN 0 356 16030 0 pbk

Macdonald & Co (Publishers) Ltd
Greater London House
Hampstead Road
London NW1 7QX

Hearing

Written by Angela Littler

Illustrated by Corinne Burrows

Macdonald

My ear

This is my ear. It catches sounds for me.

It feels bendy and has no bones. The bendy stuff is called cartilage.

Part of my ear is inside my head. You cannot see that part. It is the place that hurts when I get earache.

My ear has hairs and wax inside it to stop dirt and insects getting in.

My ear-lobe is just made out of skin and nothing else. Feel your ear-lobe and see.

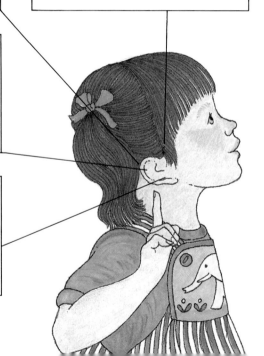

I can hear sounds with
my eyes shut;
and I can tell where the
sounds come from.

But if I can only hear
through one ear;
I do not know where
the sound is coming
from. Try it yourself.

5

Animal ears

I cannot move my ears, but many animals can. It helps them tell quickly where sounds are coming from. Dogs and cats can move their ears.

Which of these animals can move their ears?

rabbit   mouse   bird

A. The rabbit and the mouse. The bird has just slits for ears, under its feathers.

Look at all these different ears. Find the ears which look most like yours. Which animal has no outside ears?

sheepdog	poodle	pig
elephant	cat	fish
chimpanzee	bat	hamster

A: The fish. Its ears are inside its head. The slits on its head are gills, used for breathing.

Sounds that bring messages

Sometimes the sounds I hear give me messages.
Here are some pictures of things that make
special sounds

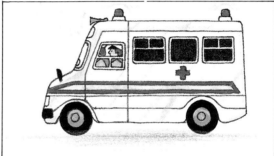

9

A sound story

When you see a picture, make the sound.

Once I went for a walk in the countryside.

A gentle breeze was blowing the clouds along

and the birds were singing happily in the trees.

Suddenly, I heard rain begin to pitter-patter on the leaves.

The wind began to blow hard through the trees.

Then lightning began to flash and the thunder boomed around me. ►

I was wet and cold and my teeth began to chatter. ►

I thought of my nice, warm house and I began to cry. ►

But just then, the wind died down, the rain stopped and the sun came out. ►

I was so happy I burst out laughing ►

and went back home, singing all the way. ►

A noisy picture

There are ten sounds in this picture. Can you spot them? Make each sound as you see it.

Which do you think is the loudest noise?
Which noise do you like best?
Which noise do you hate?

Listen to all the sounds around you wherever you are. Do it now. How many sounds can you hear?

A: The sounds in the picture are: jet aeroplane, police car siren, bird singing, cassette recorder playing music, baby crying, man hammering, child 'whooping' as an American Indian, child playing tom-tom, dog barking, a pneumatic drill.

Sound mimes

Try and tell this story to a friend by miming what is going on:

The Cat

I was driving in my car when I saw a cat in front of me. I honked my horn and put my foot on the brake. The car screeched to a halt. The cat ran off. I was pleased. I drove on.

Now try and tell it using sounds and mime but not words. Here are some sounds to use: miaow, broo-oom, honk, ee-ee-ee.

Make up some sound mimes of your own.

Deaf people

Hearing aids help many deaf people to hear better. Sometimes, deaf people also learn to lip-read. But this is very difficult to do.

Many deaf people learn sign language. They make special signs with their hands, instead of making words with their voices.

It is very hard to learn how to talk if you cannot hear anything. You cannot hear how the words should sound. You cannot hear the sounds you are making.

If you have a deaf friend, remember to face them when you speak. It is easier for them to understand what you say.

15

Making music

Would you like to make some musical sounds? Here's how:

1. A Guitar

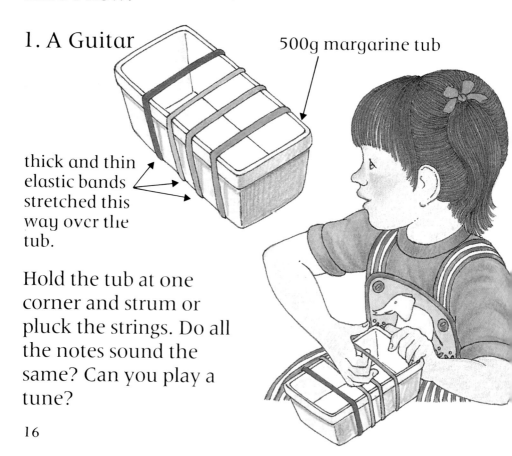

500g margarine tub

thick and thin elastic bands stretched this way over the tub.

Hold the tub at one corner and strum or pluck the strings. Do all the notes sound the same? Can you play a tune?

2.   A Trumpet

You can make a trumpet out of a cardboard tube from a roll of kitchen paper.

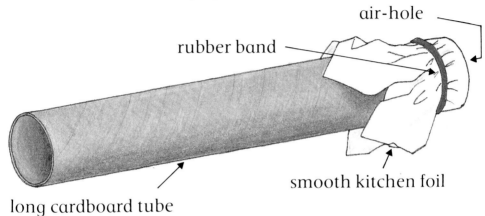

air-hole

rubber band

smooth kitchen foil

long cardboard tube

Put some new, smooth kitchen foil over the end of the tube. Fix it there with a rubber band. Pop the sharp end of a pencil *once* through the foil. This makes an air-hole. Now toot down the tube to make a loud, tinny trumpet sound.

Ask a friend to strum your home-made guitar along with you while you play.

3. Comb Music

You can make tinny music with a clean comb and a smooth piece of kitchen foil.

Cut a piece of foil about as long as the comb, but a bit taller.

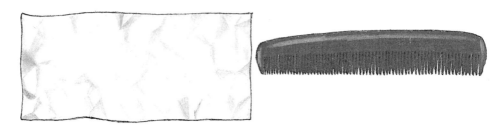

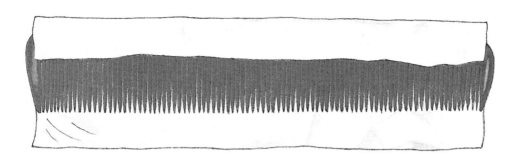

Fold a flap of foil over the top of the comb, to keep foil and comb together.

Hold the comb carefully at the very tips of each end, and put the comb side to your mouth. Then make a tune. Sing with a 'da da da' noise and you will make a good, loud sound.

The story of Quacker Duck

Several people can read this story aloud. One person reads the words, and the others make the animal noises.

Quacker Duck lived on a farm. He had a duck pond with an island of his own, and lots of friends. There was Chewy Cow who said "MOO!", Bones the Dog who said "WOOF!", Harry Horse who said "NEIGH!" and Kitty Cat who said "MIAOW!". Quacker always said "QUACK! QUACK!".

There were lots of hens, too. They said "CLUCK! CLUCK!" all day long. Quacker liked the hens, even though they could not really fly, and they could not swim. All they did was lay eggs. This made the farmer very pleased with them. But all he ever said to Quacker was:

"You're a noisy little duck, aren't you?"

The farmer and the animals had one big enemy, Slinky Fox. Slinky Fox liked eating hens' eggs, and he liked eating hens even better. Every time

he came slinking round the farm, Chewy Cow shouted "MOO!", Bones the Dog shouted "WOOF!", Harry Horse shouted "NEIGH!", and Kitty Cat shouted "MIAOW!". Quacker Duck always shouted loudest of all "QUACK! QUACK!". Then the farmer came and chased Slinky Fox away.

One evening Quacker found himself all alone on his pond. Suddenly, he saw Slinky Fox making straight for the hens.

There was no Chewy Cow to shout "MOO!". There was no Bones the Dog to shout "WOOF!". There was no Harry Horse to shout "NEIGH!" and there was no Kitty Cat to shout "MIAOW!". There was only Quacker, to shout loudest of all "QUACK! QUACK!".

The farmer ran up and chased Slinky Fox away.

"Well done!" said the farmer to Quacker. "You have saved my hens. I see that sometimes it can be useful to be noisy."

And all Quacker said was "QUACK! QUACK!".